Nelson

Handwriti

The Nelson Handwriting Font

Teacher's Guide

Christalla Watson and Janet Cassidy

Text © Christalla Watson and Janet Cassidy 2004
Introduction taken from *Nelson Handwriting Teacher's Book* by Anita Warwick,
Series editor: John Jackman

Published in 2004 by:
Nelson Thornes Ltd
Delta Place
27 Bath Road
CHELTENHAM
GL53 7TH
United Kingdom

05 06 07 08 / 10 9 8 7 6 5 4 3 2

A catalogue record for this book is available from the British Library

ISBN 0 7487 9359 3

CD-ROM and Teacher's Guide
ISBN 0 7487 9255 4

Page make-up by Green House Design, Bookham, Surrey

Printed in Great Britain by Antony Rowe

Acknowledgements

The publishers would like to thank the pupils and teachers at
Woodside Primary School, Goff's Oak, Hertfordshire for allowing
them to photograph pupils at work.
Photographs by Simon May.

ONTENTS

INTRODUCTION

The *Nelson Handwriting* scheme is now in its fifth edition, and is based on a tried and trusted font used by schools all over the UK. *The Nelson Handwriting Font* has been developed to give you the flexibility to create your own classroom resources, tailored to the needs of your class, to supplement your handwriting teaching and embed good handwriting practice across the curriculum. Moreover, The Font is straight-forward enough to be used by pupils to present their own work, and to be used on an interactive whiteboard. This is particularly effective as the Cursive fonts join in real time as you type each letter.

The Nelson Handwriting Font supports all the different fonts and features used in the *Nelson Handwriting* scheme. These include:

- Precursive
- Dotted Precursive
- Cursive
- Cursive Slanted
- Print
- Dotted Print
- Grey Text with Start Dots
- Tramlines
- Print and Cursive f and k options

This means *The Nelson Handwriting Font* can be used across the school by all teachers, who can access the font style and size which meets the needs of their class, while maintaining consistency in letter formation and joining techniques.

How to use this guide

This *Teacher's Guide* is divided into the following two sections:

Nelson Handwriting – The Basics

This provides an introduction to *The Nelson Handwriting Font* and how the scheme itself works. There is also general information and advice on developing handwriting skills, which has been taken from the most recent edition of *Nelson Handwriting Teacher's Book*.

Using the Nelson Handwriting Font

This offers advice on how to use *The Nelson Handwriting Font* and ideas on how it can support your handwriting teaching. There are hints and tips for each key stage, as well as some specific activity ideas which support handwriting, and other areas of the curriculum. This section contains many references to resource sheets and wordlists. These have been prepared for you to support these activities, and are available to download from www.nelsonthornes.com/nelson handwritingfont.

Resource sheets

Resource Sheets 1-6	**Templates for activity sheets** Taken from Nelson Handwriting Resources and Assessment books.
Resource Sheet 7	**Name Badge Layout** A bank of common children's names in outline format, enlarged and placed in a table.
Resource Sheet 8	**Gross Motor Skill Patterns** Basic patterns enlarged and set on tramlines with space for children to continue. These are in order of development.
Resource Sheet 9	**Enlarged Alphabet Cards** Each letter in outline format, enlarged to fill an A4 page.
Resource Sheet 10	**Alphabet Cards** Alphabet set out in grid to be cut out as cards for games.
Resource Sheet 11	**Bingo Card** Bingo grid with some joins in an example.
Resource Sheet 12	**Joining Sets** Enlarged letters organised in Sets 1-4 and break letters.

Wordlists

Wordlist 1	**NLS Words** High Frequency Words R-Y2.
Wordlist 2	**Numeracy Words**
Wordlist 3	**Classroom Words** Including classroom words, colours, calendar, seasons and weather words.
Wordlist 4	**Children's Names** Boy and Girl names in a grid.
Wordlist 5	**Handwriting Words** Handwriting patterns. Words containing the 4 joins – 20 words per join.

Please note that this book is not intended as a comprehensive guide to teaching handwriting skills. It provides an overview of the philosophy that underpins the *Nelson Handwriting* scheme, and creative ideas for using *The Nelson Handwriting Font* to support your teaching.

For guidance on installation, please consult the booklet supplied with the CD-ROM.

Components chart

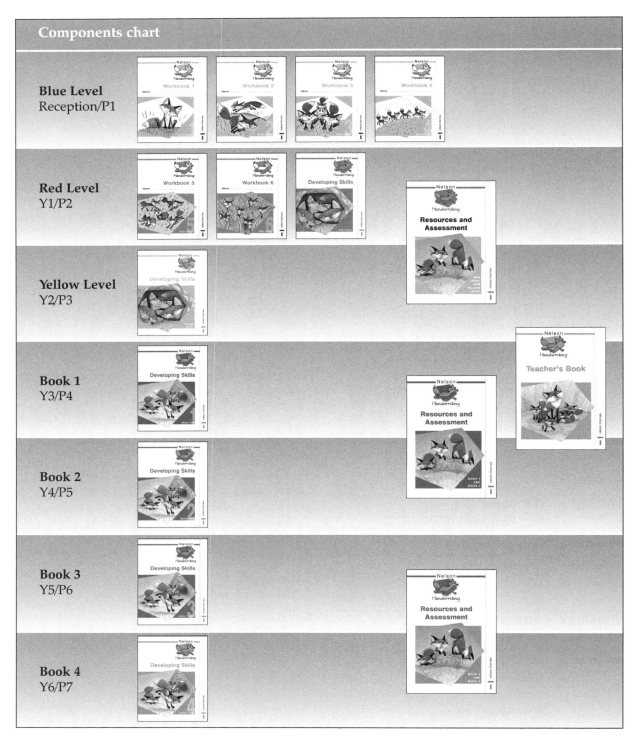

Blue Level
Reception/P1

Workbook 1 | Workbook 2 | Workbook 3 | Workbook 4

Red Level
Y1/P2

Workbook 5 | Workbook 6 | Developing Skills

Resources and Assessment

Yellow Level
Y2/P3

Developing Skills

Book 1
Y3/P4

Developing Skills

Resources and Assessment

Teacher's Book

Book 2
Y4/P5

Developing Skills

Book 3
Y5/P6

Developing Skills

Resources and Assessment

Book 4
Y6/P7

Developing Skills

Handwriting Skills

Workbooks						Developing Skills					
1	2	3	4	5	6	Red	Yellow	1	2	3	4
Handwriting patterns Pencil control	Hand-eye co-ordination Presentation										
	Letter formation (lower case)		Overwriting								
		Numerals									
			Capitals Underwriting Word spacing	Full stops Sentences Letter spacing							
				Copywriting from a model							
				The four joins and the break letters					Fluency		
							Printing				
								Writing with a slope Decorated capitals Punctuation			
									Speedwriting		
										Presentation Paragraphs Individual style Difficult joins	
											Hand-writing for different purposes

This chart shows the progression of the *Nelson Handwriting* scheme. *The Nelson Handwriting Font* can be used to support handwriting teaching at any of these stages.

The letter forms

The lower-case alphabet used in *Nelson Handwriting* Workbooks 1–4. This is available as Precursive Font with Print f and k options.

a b c d e f g h i j k l m
n o p q r s t u v w x y z

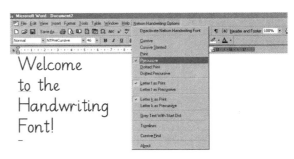

The lower-case alphabet used in *Nelson Handwriting* Developing Skills books, Resources and Assessment books Red, Yellow, 1, 2, 3, 4 and Workbooks 5 and 6. This is available as Precursive Font.

a b c d e f g h i j k l m
n o p q r s t u v w x y z

A letter with a slope from the vertical to the right is introduced in *Nelson Handwriting Developing Skills Book 1*. This is available as Cursive Slanted Font.

a b c d e f g h i j k l m
n o p q r s t u v w x y z

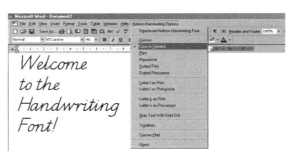

The lower-case print alphabet. This is available as Print Font.

a b c d e f g h i j k l m
n o p q r s t u v w x y z

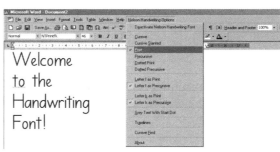

The capital letters.

A B C D E F G H I J K L M N
O P Q R S T U V W X Y Z

These are the same throughout the scheme.

The numerals.

1 2 3 4 5 6 7 8 9 0

The joining sets

Set 1

a c d e h i k l m
n s t u

Twelve letters with exit flicks plus s.

Set 2

a c d e g i j m n o
p q r s u v w x y

Nineteen letters which start at the top of the x-height.

Set 3

b f h k l t

Six letters which start at the top of the ascender.

Set 4

f o r v w

Five letters which finish at the top of the x-height.

The break letters

b g j p q x y z

Eight letters after which no join is made. Joins are not made to or from the letter z.

The joins

	Set	Set		
The first join	1 →	2	in	am
The second join	1 →	3	ab	ch
The third join	4 →	2	oa	wo
The fourth join	4 →	3	wh	ob
The break letters			bigger	

The Cursive style

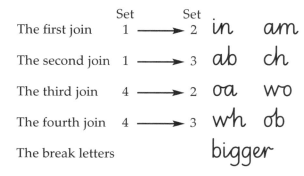

The Cursive Slanted style

3 TEACHING METHODS AND ORGANISATION

The role of the teacher

There is no single formula for success in the teaching of handwriting, but some basic principles are identifiable:

- Handwriting lessons should be in line with school policy.
- As handwriting is a movement skill, demonstration by a competent teacher is essential.
- When children practise using models from the *Nelson Handwriting* materials, teachers should observe them carefully and be ready to intervene with support and encouragement.
- In the early stages of learning to write, the process is more important than the product. Irregular letter forms starting in the correct place with movement in the correct direction are to be preferred to uniformly regular letters achieved through wrong movements.
- Every effort should be made to prevent significant faults becoming ingrained habits that will be difficult to break.

  Common faults include: faulty pencil/pen grip, incorrect letter formation, reversals and inversions, poor posture and paper positioning.

Raising children's awareness of key points

The teacher's role in raising children's awareness of the technical aspects of handwriting is essential. *Nelson Handwriting* provides a clear development structure for teachers to refer to through demonstration and discussion.

Terminology

As teachers demonstrate the skills of handwriting, it is important to describe the movements involved. Many teachers have developed their own user-friendly descriptors which are age-appropriate. However, there are some technical terms which are so useful in discussion about handwriting that it is important for pupils to understand them.

These include: *clockwise, anticlockwise, vertical, horizontal, diagonal, parallel, ascender, descender, consonant, vowel, joined, sloped, x-height*.
See **Wordlist 5, Handwriting Words** for labels featuring these words.

Whole-class and group teaching

To some extent the decision about whether to take handwriting lessons with individuals, groups or whole classes is a matter of personal preference. However, the varied developmental stages of pupils and the need for sensible economy of time and effort also influence practice. Consider the following suggestions:

- In the early stages, it is appropriate to give handwriting lessons to small groups of children with similar levels of readiness and motor control. Individuals within each group may require specific help.
- Later on, as children come to understand the concept of written language and show evidence of developing control, it may be economical to work with large groups and whole classes.

Regular practice

In primary schools where class teachers are generally responsible for teaching handwriting to their own classes, there are many opportunities to practise the skills of handwriting in the course of writing across the curriculum. However, it is also necessary to provide regular lessons for the teaching and/or revision of handwriting skills.

The frequency and length of handwriting lessons is likely to vary according to the age and competence of the pupils. With young children it is appropriate to have short, daily lessons, while older pupils may benefit from one or two longer sessions each week.

The amount of time devoted to handwriting may also depend on the point reached in the programme. For example, it may be helpful to provide extra lessons when joins are being introduced.

Writing materials

Tools

Throughout the school, children should be encouraged to experience writing with different tools. Pens, pencils, chalks and crayons should be available for them to experiment with. In the early stages, a soft pencil with a thick stem may be most appropriate. Too thin a pencil, offered too soon, may result in a tight grip. The standard pencil should be introduced as a child's motor skills begin to improve. At the beginning of junior school a child's main writing tool will probably be a standard pencil, although some schools allow the use of ballpoint pens.

At some point, schools will encourage children to write in ink, using a fountain pen or something similar. It is best to avoid the use of fine-pointed nibs.

Paper

In the early stages, children should be encouraged to make free-flowing movements and to produce large patterns, letters and words on large sheets of plain paper (or on an interactive whiteboard). In The *Nelson Handwriting Font*, guidlines can be generated using the tramlines facility. As their motor skills increase, the size of the writing should decrease and exercise books can then be used for handwriting practice. The *Nelson Handwriting* Workbooks provide a structured introduction to letter formation, giving guidance on shape and directional flow. Guidelines are provided in the Workbooks and in the Resource sheets accompanying *Developing Skills Red* and *Yellow Level* and *Book 1*. These help children to appreciate the relative proportions of letters and to understand how to position them.

Throughout their schooling, all children should be encouraged to use unlined paper from time to time. This allows them to determine letter size, spacing and the arrangement of the page, and to consider other issues of aesthetics and presentation.

Getting ready to write

Atmosphere

Try to create a relaxed atmosphere. Wrist-shaking exercises, scribbling and practising writing patterns all help to loosen up muscles ready for writing.

Seating and posture

The child's chair and table should be at a comfortable height. The table should support the forearm so that it rests lightly on the surface and is parallel to the floor. Children should be encouraged to sit up straight and not to slouch. The height of the chair should be such that the thighs are horizontal and the feet flat on the floor. Tables should be free of clutter and there should be adequate light to allow children to see what they are doing. Ideally, left-handed pupils should sit on the left of their partners so that their movements are not restricted.

Pencil and pen grip

'Pupils should be taught to hold a pencil comfortably.' (England and Wales: *English in the National Curriculum*)

For all children, especially left-handers, a pen or pencil with a rounded nib or point is best for writing.

For right-handers a tripod grip is generally accepted as the most efficient way of holding a pen or pencil. It should be held lightly between the thumb and forefinger about 3 cm from the point. The middle finger provides additional support. The book or writing paper should be placed to the right, tilted slightly to the left. The left hand should be used to steady the paper.

Left-handers are in a minority, and our writing system favours the right-hander. Left-handers therefore need plenty of encouragement and support. When a left-hander makes joining strokes they are pushed, not pulled as they are by a right-hander. Encourage them to hold their pencils far enough away from the point to allow them to see what they are writing. The tripod grip should be much the same as for a right-hander. The book or paper should be positioned to the left and tilted slightly to the right.

Encourage children to refer to the checklist on the back of the flap at the front of each *Developing Skills* book to help them to prepare for writing. An example of this is on page 14. A left-hand version of the flap is available in the accompanying *Resources and Assessment* books.

The writing process and the *Nelson Handwriting* scheme

Handwriting patterns
Pupils should use material 'to develop hand-eye co-ordination'. (Scotland: *English 5–14 Guidelines*)

Writing patterns that reinforce basic handwriting movements will help to develop fluency, control and confidence. Patterns are provided throughout *Nelson Handwriting*, and children should be encouraged to use a variety of writing implements to complete them. There are guidelines on generating patterns with *The Nelson Handwriting Font* on page 25.

Focus
Each handwriting lesson should have a clear focus. This should be discussed, and demonstrations given to emphasise key teaching points. Each unit in the *Developing Skills* books begins with a Focus section.

Practice
Pupils should have opportunities for 'purposeful, guided practice'. (Northern Ireland: *English Programmes of Study and Attainment Targets*)

Motivated and directed handwriting practice is essential. The focus of each unit of work in the *Developing Skills* books is followed by purposeful practice of a specific handwriting skill. Focus and Extension Resource Sheets allow for further practice at the pupil's own level.

Writing for a purpose
'Pupils should gain experience across a wide variety of forms.' (Scotland: *English 5–14 Guidelines*)

Pupils should be taught 'to use different forms of writing for different purposes'. (England and Wales: *English in the National Curriculum*)

All the exercises in *Nelson Handwriting* are designed to be interesting and enjoyable, and are relevant to the curriculum wherever possible. The activities are designed to reinforce key English skills in spelling, grammar, vocabulary and punctuation and care has been taken to complement the work in *Nelson English* and *Nelson Spelling*.

Children should be taught to adapt their writing according to the requirements of the task. In *Nelson Handwriting*, they are taught a print script in *Developing Skills Yellow Level* and are encouraged to use it in a variety of situations, e.g. for labelling maps and diagrams. (Print font is available in *The Nelson Handwriting Font*.) They are also taught to write quickly, without losing legibility, for making notes. The writing activities span a range of genres, including real-life writing situations.

Fluency and rhythm
Pupils should be expected to 'develop greater control and fluency'. (England and Wales: *English in the National Curriculum*)

Fluent handwriting is writing in which the pencil literally flows from letter to letter in a smooth and almost continuous process. Children should be encouraged to write at a reasonable speed in order to develop this skill. Handwriting patterns are a useful aid in this respect. (see **Resource Sheet 8, Gross Motor Skill Patterns**)

Speed
The essential qualities of good writing are fluency, neatness and speed. Fluency is best achieved at speed, but writing done too quickly often suffers from loss of form, regularity and legibility. The Nelson Handwriting style and joining methods have been designed to stand up to demands for speedy, efficient handwriting. Activities to develop speed writing in the scheme are provided from *Developing Skills Book 1*, together with tests enabling children to work out their own writing speed.

Individuality

Children should not be expected to make exact reproductions of the letter forms presented as models in *Nelson Handwriting*. In due course it is likely that many children will develop individual variations on this style. These variations will give their writing character and, provided that the writing is legible, are to be encouraged. In *Developing Skills Book 3 and 4* children are actively encouraged to explore different styles of handwriting.

Presentation

Pupils should develop an awareness of the 'importance of clear, neat presentation, in order to communicate their meaning effectively'. (England and Wales: *English in the National Curriculum*)

Children need to learn to consider the visual impact of their writing as well as its accuracy. Aspects of presentation (including spacing, margins, borders, illustration and calligraphic effects) are focused on throughout the course.

Not every occasion warrants 'best' writing. It is more helpful for children to write with a degree of care, at an appropriate speed, for most normal purposes, so that their writing is legible and fluent and not too painstakingly produced. 'Best' writing can be reserved for those occasions when attention can be concentrated on the mechanical skills of writing and when there is seen to be a clear purpose for producing aesthetically pleasing work. Older children should be helped to realise that some writing tasks require a draft version to be written first. Then, after revision and editing, the draft can be re-written in 'best' writing.

Some suggestions for encouraging aesthetic presentation of written work are as follows:

- Hold an annual or termly handwriting competition.
- Have a noticeboard on which frequently changed displays of good work are pinned.
- Write out work for wall displays in connection with other work being undertaken, after rough drafts have been corrected.

- Encourage children to compile individual anthologies of favourite poems and extracts which may be illustrated appropriately.
- Produce a class magazine in which individual contributions are handwritten.
- Produce handwritten, decorated programmes for bazaars, concerts and parents' evenings.
- Ask children to decorate their work with writing patterns.
- Encourage children to experiment with different ways of presenting writing:
  - a poem or narrative which forms a shape relating to its subject,
  - curved or spiral writing,
  - decorated capitals,
  - writing in coloured ink,
  - writing over illustrations which have been lightly coloured,
  - experimenting with the relationship between writing and illustration.

Handwriting across the curriculum

There are many opportunities to practise the skills of handwriting during the course of lessons in other subjects.

Research has confirmed the natural link between spelling and handwriting. The examples used in *Nelson Handwriting* consolidate pupils' mastery of common spelling rules and develop both a visual and a motor memory of spelling patterns.

The Nelson Handwriting Font gives you the opportunity to embed handwriting within your spelling work and across other areas of the curriculum.

5 ASSESSMENT

It is important to establish ways of assessing handwriting at several levels:

- whole-school assessment,
- class assessment,
- individual assessment,
- self-assessment.

Whole-school and class assessment

From time to time it is useful to confirm that the school or class handwriting policy is effective. A regular survey of children's writing allows for a general, impressionistic assessment and may indicate the need for a more detailed investigation. This kind of monitoring of school-wide standards is most likely to occur if one member of staff is responsible for starting the process at regular intervals and ensuring that any weaknesses or problems are followed up. Criteria might include:

- Is the writing generally legible and pleasant?
- Are the letters correctly shaped and proportioned?
- Are the joins made correctly?
- Are the spaces between letters, words and lines appropriate?
- Is the size of the writing appropriate?
- Is the writing properly aligned?
- Are the writing standards achieved by the majority of pupils in line with the Level Descriptors of the statutory curricula?

Appropriate assessment materials are provided in the *Resources and Assessment* books which accompany the *Developing Skills* books.

Individual assessment

To assess the progress of individual children it is necessary to observe them as they write, as well as studying their finished writing. Criteria for individual assessments include:

- Does the child adopt the correct posture?
- Does the child hold the pen/pencil correctly?
- Does the child use the correct movement when forming and/or joining letters?
- Does the child reverse or invert any letters?

- Does the child write fluently and rhythmically?
- Is the writing easily legible?
- Is the writing appropriate?
- Is the pupil's handwriting development in line with the Level Descriptors of the statutory curricula?

Each *Developing Skills* book contains Check-ups to assess the individual progress of each child. Each *Resources and Assessment* book contains an assessment section with resource sheets designed to be used as placement tests, general assessment and self-assessment.

The 'Getting ready to write' flap at the front of each *Developing Skills* book (as shown below) is intended to remind pupils about how to prepare themselves for writing. The checklist on the reverse of this gives a list of criteria to help pupils focus on, and check critically, particular aspects of the writing they have done. Throughout the *Developing Skills* books, children are frequently reminded to assess their own writing and this checklist will help them. The checklist may also be used as a basis for pairs of pupils to discuss each other's writing, or as a basis for a handwriting conference between teacher and child.

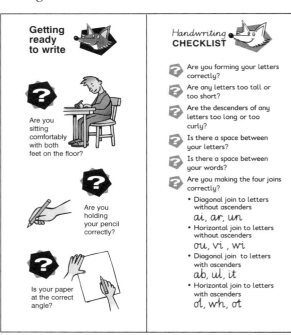

Level Descriptors in the statutory curricula

England and Wales

Level 1 'Letters are usually clearly shaped and correctly oriented.'

Level 2 'In handwriting, letters are accurately formed and consistent in size.'

Level 3 'Handwriting is joined and legible.'

Level 4 'Handwriting style is fluent, joined and legible.'

Level 5 'Handwriting is joined clear and fluent and, where appropriate, is adapted to a range of tasks.'

Scotland

Level A In writing tasks pupils 'form letters and space words legibly for the most part. At an appropriate stage, linkage of letters will be taught.'

Level B In writing tasks pupils 'form letters and space words legibly in linked script'.

Level C In writing tasks pupils 'employ a fluent, legible style of handwriting'.

Level D In writing tasks pupils 'employ a fluent, legible style of handwriting and set out completed work giving attention to presentation and layout'.

Level E In writing tasks pupils 'employ a fluent, legible style of handwriting, and set out completed work clearly and attractively'.

Northern Ireland

Level 1 'Pupils should show some control over the size, shape and orientation of letters.'

Level 2 'There is evidence of the use of upper and lower case letters.'

Level 3 'Handwriting is accurately formed and consistant in size.'

Level 4 'Handwriting is swift and legible.'

Level 5 'Handwriting is swift and legible.'

Specific handwriting difficulties

Some problems and possible solutions
Faulty pencil grip
An over-tight pencil grip is the most common fault. Crooking of the forefinger and pressing too hard are common indications of this. Encourage the pupil to relax and to hold the pencil lightly between the thumb and the middle finger, while the forefinger rests lightly on the pencil.

Incorrect letter formation
Children are often able to write letters which are correctly shaped but which have been produced by incorrect movements. If bad habits of this kind are allowed to become ingrained, the child will be seriously hampered when he or she progresses to joined writing. It is important, in the early stages of development, to ensure that:

• all letters are started in the correct place,
• in general, movements start at the top and go down,
• ovals are made with an anticlockwise movement.

Reversal, inversions and mirror writing
Common problems include:

• reversal: b for d and p for q,
• inversions: w for m,
• mirror writing: was for saw.

Causes include:

• confusion between left and right,
• a lack of commitment to one hand,
• a natural tendency for left-handers to pull the hand across the body from right to left, thus causing confusion,
• a general lack of maturity or confidence.

Children with these problems can be helped by increased emphasis on the writing direction and the consistent use of one hand for writing.

Pen hold

The left-handed, like the right-handed child, needs to be shown as early as possible how to hold a writing implement correctly. Bad habits are easily learnt and many left-handers adopt a hooked pencil hold which can result in a tired grip and affect the quality of their writing. When they begin to use a pen their hand can easily smudge the ink as they write.

If a child already has a 'hooked' pencil hold, do not force them to change. It is very difficult to alter the way you have learnt to hold a pencil, and confidence can easily be destroyed. Encourage them *instead* to angle their paper 20–30° to the left, i.e. the same angle used for a right-handed child. If possible, demonstrate how to hold a pen and how to form and join letters with your left hand.

The left-hander should hold the pencil in the left hand in the same way as a right-handed person holds theirs. The pencil is held between thumb and forefinger, resting on the first knuckle of the middle finger. The pencil should be held about 3 cm from the tip.

The hand should be kept below the writing line. This enables the children to see what they are writing and encourages correct pen hold.

The grip the left-hander uses means the pencil is pushed as the child writes, whereas the right-hander pulls their pencil across the page as they write. It is important therefore that the left-hander's pencil is not too sharp, so that it will run smoothly across the page.

Paper position

The left-hander will find it easier if the paper is tilted slightly to the right, at about 20–30°. The higher the angle the harder it is for most children to write efficiently. The right hand is used to steady the paper, above the writing line.

Crossing letters

The left-hander often crosses the 'f' and 't' from right to left. Many left-handers therefore will find it easier to leave the 'f' unjoined.

Teachers need to be aware of left-handers in the classroom as they do have different needs. It is very important that a right-handed child is not seated on the left-hand side of a left-handed child as their elbows will collide!

7 LINKING HANDWRITING AND SPELLING

The English National Curriculum includes the requirement that:

In spelling, pupils should be taught to: write each letter of the alphabet; use their knowledge of sound–symbol relationships and phonological patterns; recognise and use simple spelling patterns; write common letter strings within familiar and common words;

Indeed, a balanced spelling programme would be incomplete without techniques for stimulating visual memory and, as has been recognised for generations, the classic way of achieving this is to integrate the learning of spelling with the development of handwriting; one of the most powerful methods of stimulating the visual memory.

Remembering the feeling of tracing the shapes of letters is important in the early stages of handwriting. This too can be part of the early spelling programme.

Nelson Handwriting provides a progressive, carefully graded programme of activities, based around phonically regular words, ensuring that in parallel with the important regular handwriting practice, the children are undertaking meaningful spelling tasks. If handwriting is practised using letters in regular combinations, be they blends, strings or digraphs, then young writers will begin to internalise the patterns and increase both their handwriting and spelling ability and confidence.

Given the pressures and time constraints in the average modern classroom, it has to make good classroom management sense to integrate handwriting and spelling whenever possible.

Look – Say – Cover – Write – Check

The child:
Looks at the word very carefully, including how the letters join.

Says the word.

Covers the word so that it can't be seen.

Writes the whole word from memory, saying it softly as they write, taking care both to spell the word correctly and to join the letters correctly.

Checks what has been written. If they have not written the word correctly, or have not joined the letters correctly, they go back and repeat all these steps again.

Once the child has learnt to spell a new word correctly, they write it into their wordbooks. Even if they get the spelling and the joins right first time, it is useful to practise both again.

Some children can struggle with *Look Say Cover Write Check* if left on their own, or in a small group. Initially the words they practise will be two-letter words, but later the *Look Say Cover Write Check* process can be used to correct two or three spellings from a child's piece of creative writing. *Look Say Cover Write Check* can also be linked to the school's phonic programme.

Don't forget:

- To praise and encourage the child for what they have already written. This builds confidence – confidence builds success – success builds confidence.

- To ask the child if you can show them how to write what they have written in joined-up writing.

- The child watches as the teacher writes.

School policy

An aim of every school should be to teach each child to write legibly, fluently and at reasonable speed. To achieve this schools should consider the following recommendations:

• One member of staff should have responsibility for handwriting. This responsibility should be written into that person's job description.

• This member of staff should be given time and resources to help other staff.

• The school should develop a 'whole-school approach' so that teaching is consistent and all teachers are giving the same advice to parents, visiting teachers and supply teachers.

• School policy ought to be consistent between linking key stages.

• The staff need to agree on a common approach to such things as timetabling handwriting activities, style to be adopted, implements to be allowed, involvement of parents and policy on correcting work.

The success of whole-school policies depends upon the level of ownership and understanding felt by all people whose behaviour and thinking they seek to influence. This applies equally to creating, implementing and managing a policy for handwriting. In the author's experience, a sequence of five stages may be helpful in establishing a handwriting policy.

Stage 1: Identify current practice

Ask staff to bring some examples of handwriting from their class. The examples should illustrate a range of ability levels.

In small groups, discuss current practice:

• How is handwriting currently taught in your class?

• Discuss examples of work.

• Share any difficulties, concerns, successes or issues.

• What might be the advantages of introducing joined handwriting earlier?

• What might be the disadvantages?

Report back to main group. Discuss the issues and record the results of discussion. Unresolved issues will need to be discussed at another time.

Stage 2: improving current practice

In groups discuss the following questions:

• Does the school's current approach ensure that every child achieves their full potential?

• Would more children achieve Levels 2/3 in English at the end of Key Stage 1 (or equivalent) if the school's handwriting policy was different?

• Would more children be able to write legibly, fluently and neatly with speed if they were introduced to joined writing earlier?

• Discuss and try to resolve any concerns.

• What resources do you have or need?

• Can handwriting practice be linked to spelling/phonic progression?

Feed back to main group.

Stage 3: agree an approach

• Decide on a model to use, for example the one provided by the *Nelson Handwriting* scheme.

• Agree the time allocation to be given to handwriting.

• Decide on materials that will be used and when.

Some teachers will never agree on handwriting. It is an emotive subject and many hold strong views and opinions. It may help if one person or the senior management team makes the final decision. Remind staff that the new policy can be trialled, evidence collected and a review carried out in twelve months' time.

Stage 4: draw up the policy

It helps if one person or group draws up a draft policy which can be brought to the staff and discussed.

Include in your handwriting policy:

- The model used:
  lower case letters,
  capital letters,
  numerals.

- The break letters.

- The four joins.

- The order of teaching, i.e. it is useful to group letters together based on similar movements, followed by phonic progression.

- The three 'P's:
  posture,
  pen hold,
  paper position.

- an illustration of the three 'P's,

- Advice for left-handers.

- Use of lined or unlined paper.

- Equipment used.

- Assessment and record keeping procedures.

- A small information booklet could be provided and given to parents before their child starts school (and given to supply teachers). Such a booklet should include:

- lower-case letters showing correct entry point and direction of movement,

- an example to show how letters join, e.g. a poem,

- handy hints on appropriate writing tools and paper.

A well-thought-out and consistently applied policy will benefit all the teachers and the children at your school. Continuity throughout the school enables children to build on what they have already been taught and know. It also helps eradicate confusion and avoids difficulties and problems later on.

Stage 5: review and evaluation of policy

Review and evaluation of any policy is important. It keeps both policy and guidelines alive and informs both old and new staff.

Evaluate and review your policy annually if you can. The model or style of writing you choose to adopt is not as important as the fact that you are encouraging joined handwriting with all the positive benefits it entails. Teachers need encouragement too. We don't always get the model and style correct all the time, but both pupils and staff can perfect style at a later stage.

Finally recognise, celebrate and advertise your successes!

9 TECHNIQUES FOR TEACHING LETTER FORMATION

- Provide demonstrations when introducing and teaching letter shapes. Chalkboards, OHPs and interactive whiteboards are useful for this.

- Observe individuals as much as possible while they practise. This enables the teacher to recognise and correct bad habits as they arise.

- Talk the children through the process using appropriate language.

- Encourage children to verbalise what they are doing from time to time. This gives a window into the thought processes they are using as they write.

- Writing involves visual and motor skills. Use the following ideas to reinforce the teaching of letter shapes:
    - Encourage children to form letters by drawing them in the air.
    - Finger trace over tactile letters.
    - Write over dotted or 'shadow' writing.
    - Draw round templates.
    - Write in sand with a finger or stick.
    - Write with chalk on a chalkboard.
    - Write on an interactive whiteboard.
    - Write letters boldly with a wax candle and then apply a colour wash.
    - Form letters with pegs on a pegboard or with beads in plasticine.
    - Finger trace the outline of a letter on the back of the person in front of you.
    - Form letters with fingers and/or bodies, individually and in groups.

- Draw attention to the connection between letters and the related writing patterns. Encouraging children to use the basic handwriting patterns both for practice and for decorative purposes is a valuable technique for fostering fluency and rhythmic movement.

10 THE JOINS

Joins between letters increase the speed, rhythm and ease of writing without reducing legibility.

In *Nelson Handwriting*, the 26 lower-case letters have been divided into five sets according to the nature of the joins they require. There are four types of join and a set of 'break' letters after which joins are never made. (See pages 8–9 for details of these sets of letters.)

The joins are taught in *Red Level* and practice is provided in all subsequent books.

The first join *in*

The join from any member of Set 1 to any member of Set 2 is made with exactly the same movement as the upswing in the swings pattern.

The second join *il*

The join from any member of Set 1 to any member of Set 3 is the same as the first join except that the join meets the ascender halfway up the letter and then continues to the top of the ascender.

The third join *og*

The join from any member of Set 4 to any member of Set 2 is a shallow horizontal curve because the join is from x-height of one letter to the x-height of the next.

The fourth join *ob*

The join from any member of Set 4 to any member of Set 3 is the same as the first join except that it goes from the x-height of one letter to the top of the ascender of the next.

The break letters

Joins are never made after the letters in this set.

No join is ever made to or from the letter z. A small space should be left after each break letter so that it is spaced as evenly as the joined letters.

The letters e and s have slightly varying forms because their shapes depend on the nature of the preceding join. Attention is drawn to these special cases in the *Developing Skills Red* and *Yellow Levels*.

As the size of writing decreases, children should be encouraged to decrease the space between words.

Teaching the joined style

- In the early stages the correct movements are more important than the appearance of the writing. Children should be discouraged from forming writing with incorrect movements, even if they manage to achieve results that appear satisfactory. However, in later stages a more individual style based around *Nelson Handwriting* is encouraged.

- As joined handwriting is a movement skill, it is essential for teachers to provide demonstrations. Chalkboards, OHPs and interactive whiteboards are useful for this.

- Observe individuals as much as possible while they practise. This enables the teacher to recognise and correct bad habits as they arise.

- Talk the children through the process, using appropriate language.

- Encourage children to verbalise what they are doing from time to time. This gives a window into the thought processes they are using as they write.

- Most children will need extra practice with making the joins. *The Developing Skills* and *Resources and Assessment* books provide ample material for this.

- Encouraging children to use the basic handwriting patterns both for practice and for decorative purposes is a valuable technique for fostering fluency and rhythmic movement.

GENERAL APPLICATIONS OF
THE NELSON HANDWRITING FONT

The Nelson Handwriting Font family can be used like any other font within Microsoft® Word, (using the Nelson Handwriting Word template) and offers the same flexibility. However, you now have the additional benefit of embedding good handwriting practice throughout the curriculum. There are endless possibilities for its use but here are a few general suggestions.

TAILOR-MADE WORKSHEETS

Use *The Nelson Handwriting Font* to suit the needs of individuals and groups in your class by creating your own worksheets. These can be to focus on handwriting skills in particular (the Grey Font with start dots will be especially useful for this) or simply create your own worksheets for any curriculum area and embed good handwriting practice at the same time.

• Use **Resource Sheets 1-6** supplied at www.nelsonthornes.com/nelsonhandwriting font as a template(s) for creating your own worksheets.

• Alternatively, download other online resources and copy them into *The Nelson Handwriting* template to convert them into the font of your choice. Please note, that if these documents are PDFs they cannot be converted into another font style.

• Download other texts from websites and convert the text in *The Nelson Handwriting* template. For example, provide your class with different text types or poems in the handwriting style of your choice.

• Please note, in order to change NT Cursive text to any other font, it first has to be changed to NT Precursive or NT Print.

ENVIRONMENTAL PRINT

Banners
Use *The Nelson Handwriting Font* to create banners for displays. This is particularly effective if you use the outline facility with the font to cut out display letters on card or paper to save tracing around templates. You can increase the size of the font, or enlarge printouts on a photocopier.

Labels and Captions
Produce labels and captions for your classroom in *The Nelson Handwriting Font*. See **Wordlists 1-5** for some useful vocabulary which has already been entered for you, e.g. classroom words, colours, numeracy words, weather words and children's names. The NT Print font style is particularly recommended to reinforce good handwriting practice for labels and captions.

ADDING EFFECTS TO
THE NELSON HANDWRITING FONT

Make the most of the *Nelson Handwriting* Fonts by adding text effects or using Microsoft® *WordArt* and *AutoShapes*.

Text Effects
1 Highlight the text.

2 Click *Format* then *Font*.

3 Under *Effects*, tick the effect you'd like and click *OK*.

Try giving text an outline

WordArt
1 Open the Drawing toolbar by clicking *View*, then *Toolbars* and tick *Drawing*.

2 Click on the *WordArt* icon in the toolbar (a blue A).

3 Select the style of *WordArt*, click 'OK' and then enter your text as indicated.

4 Scroll through the font options and select NT Precursive or NT Print (please note the joined fonts DO NOT work in *WordArt*).

5 Text will appear in your word document, for example:

AutoShapes

1 Open the *Drawing* toolbar as described above.

2 Click on the *AutoShapes* tab and select *Callouts*. This will reveal a selection of textboxes in useful creative shapes like speech and thought bubbles, or captions.

3 Select the shape of your choice, and the cursor will change into a drawing tool.

4 Click somewhere on the page and drag the mouse to create the shape in whatever size you need. Release the mouse at the desired size, and the shape will sit on your page with the associated properties of a text box.

5 Although you can type straight into this shape, if you want to use any of the joined fonts, we recommend typing the text first and then pasting it into the shape.

6 Select and paste the text you want to put in this shape.

7 Try using other shapes from this menu, remember you can enlarge these on the photocopier for displays.

Save time with your displays!

A COLLABORATIVE HANDWRITING DISPLAY

Create a handwriting display for the classroom, which will be a useful reminder of the joins and the importance of good handwriting. Depending on the ICT ability level of the children, involve them in this process too. Use *The Nelson Handwriting Font*, and the children's own examples of handwriting styles to produce a class display.

It may be useful to display:

- a reminder of joins between sets (See page 21 for these),

- NT Cursive grey font, showing where to start each break letter,

- prompts for 'Getting ready to write' (See page 14 for these),

- handwriting vocabulary,

- a handwriting checklist (See page 14 for this),

- examples of good handwriting by the children,

- different handwriting styles collected.

PUBLISHING SUPPORT FOR SEN PUPILS

Encourage the children to word process their finished pieces of writing in *The Nelson Handwriting Font*. Alternatively, for SEN children, prepare some of the children's writing in *The Nelson Handwriting Font* for them, so that they can then use it as a guide to practise their neatest handwriting. By doing this, you can control how much editing you want the children to do and the particular focus of their editing and publishing work.

USE *THE NELSON HANDWRITING FONT* ON OHP OR INTERACTIVE WHITEBOARD

Use *The Nelson Handwriting Font* to make OHTs or on an interactive whiteboard to encourage gross motor skills (See **Resource Sheet 8, Gross Motor Skills Patterns**), and introduce shapes, patterns or joins to the class. There are specific whiteboard activities for each key stage in this guide. Here are some general guidelines:

- To annotate diagrams, images or key text on the interactive whiteboard, you first have to paste that image into Microsoft® Word and then you

Using an interactive whiteboard.

can use the font in any style and with all the Microsoft® Word functionality.

- To use the whiteboard tools in conjunction with the NT Font, for example to encourage children to trace over letter shapes or patterns with their hand or whiteboard pen, prepare the activity in Microsoft® Word first. This avoids having to switch between the Microsoft® Word and the interactive whiteboard functionalities, e.g. Active Studio.

USING THE NELSON HANDWRITING FONT ON A TABLET PC

If you have access to Tablet PCs, encourage the use of *The Nelson Handwriting Font* to focus on handwriting skills. Many of the activities listed in this book would be ideal, but in addition to demonstrating and practising joins, you are able to support children to grip the pencil correctly and angle the 'paper' correctly.

WORD PROCESSING

Encourage the children to explore *The Nelson Handwriting Font* options when they are drafting, editing and publishing their own work. It is simple to use and offers an attractive alternative to the standard suite of Fonts.

CREATE WRITING FRAMES – ON AN INTERACTIVE WHITEBOARD OR OHT

You can use *The Nelson Handwriting Font* to create writing frames for a particular purpose. It provides good opportunity to:

- customise writing frames to suit your needs.

- allow the children to come and add their own ideas to the writing frame in their own handwriting, practising the joins.

- experiment with different fonts and the impact these have on the article and reader. (Please note, in order to change NT Cursive text to any other font, it first has to be changed to NT Precursive or NT Print.)

HINTS AND TIPS

 Exploring shapes and patterns

You could create a selection of activity sheets which focus on any of the patterns that the children are exploring at the time. *The Nelson Handwriting Font* allows you to make these as big as you wish to encourage gross motor skill development. You can also enlarge these to A3 size on the photocopier.

Try leaving these on the writing table for children to access freely. Alternatively, create a range of small workbooks with tramlines for the children to write in, with and without letters on them.

See **Resource Sheets 1-6** as examples or use these as templates to design your own.

 High frequency word walls and tricky word walls

Set up a display featuring tricky words or high frequency words printed in the appropriate font option. Add new words to this display as the children discover them and encourage them to use this display as a resource. See **Wordlist 1, NLS Words** for high frequency vocabulary that has been entered for you.

 Talking walls

To improve specific vocabulary in speaking and listening, create a poster to display the words you are focusing on that week/month/term. This will be a useful reminder for all the adults to reinforce these words in their talk with the children.

Sound and word walls

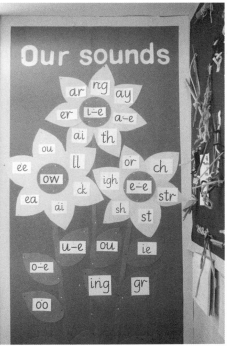

Table reminders

Ask the children to type the alphabet in lower case and then upper case underneath, or prepare this yourself. Print and laminate these strips and stick them to the tables for children to use as support when they are writing.

Use the Grey font so that the children can see the start dots and directional arrows to help them to form their letters.

 Dictionaries

Use *The Nelson Handwriting Font* to make a simple dictionary for each child. On each page have the letter and a picture of something starting with that letter. Then copy ten sets of tramlines and have the letter, e.g. **a**, written at the start of each line ready to be traced and other letters added to spell words beginning with **a**. You could ask the children to find five new words to put in their book every week, one every night and a picture to match the word. When they are in class they can use their dictionaries to help them with their independent writing.

ACTIVITIES

1 Name badges

- To develop a comfortable pencil grip and to write letters using the correct sequence of movements.

- To develop fine and gross motor skills.

- To learn to write and spell their own names.

- For the whole class, groups or individuals.

Preparation
- Make name badges for the class using the NT Precursive font in the outline format. **Resource Sheet 7, Name Badge Layout** provides a template for name badges and features common children's names.

- To create this outline, highlight the name, go to the *Format* menu, select *Font* and tick Outline in the *Effects* options. For example:

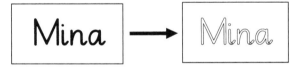

Activity
Give each child their name badge and invite them to practise writing their names within the enlarged outline. When the children can write their first names independently, provide them with badges featuring their surnames, and then progress to letting the children write their own name badges unsupported. The badges can be used yo support children when writing their names independently.

Challenge: During ICT invite the children to type their own names in the box/badge and print them out themselves.

2 Decorating letters

• To develop fine motor control

• For groups or pairs.

Preparation

• You will need a set of large (A4 or A3) alphabet cards.

• To create these enter each letter of the alphabet into Microsoft® Word in *The Nelson Handwriting Font* of your choice. Select all and go to the *Format* option on the toolbar, click *Font*, change the size to 400 point and choose the Outline option in the *Effects* menu. This has been done for you in **Resource Sheet 9, Enlarged Alphabet Cards**.

Activity

Give the children a card with a letter on it, and invite them to add glue and then fill in the outline of the letter with glitter. This will develop their pincer movement/action. Alternatively, give the children the opportunity to decorate the letters with sequins or paint, or to make play dough models of them.

Use the letters the children decorate to make a display of the alphabet, or to display particular words, such as CVC words, or days of the week. The children could build up a word/letter wall over time.

Challenge: Put the letters on a table for the children to explore and rearrange to spell new words.

3 Ball games

• To develop fine and gross motor skills.

• For individuals, groups or whole class.

Preparation

• You will need a set of large (A3) alphabet cards.

• To create these enter each letter of the alphabet into Microsoft® Word in *The Nelson Handwriting Font* of your choice. Select all and go to the *Format* option on the tool bar, click *Font*, change the size to 650 point and choose the Outline option in the *Effects* menu. This has been done for you in **Resource Sheet 9, Enlarged Alphabet Cards**.

• Enlarge them to A3 size on the photocopier and laminate them.

Activity

Ask the children to roll/control a ball around the letter shape, using the outline as a guide. As they improve their motor skills, encourage them to use a smaller ball each time, eventually trying with a marble or bean.

Challenge: When the children are competent with the enlarged letters, reduce the size of the letters and give them whole words to try.

4 Circle alphabet game

- To write letters using the correct sequence of movements.
- For whole class or group.

5 Musical letters

- To learn different letters and phonemes.
- For the whole class.

Preparation
- You will need a set of large (A4 or A3) laminated alphabet cards.
- To create these enter each letter of the alphabet into Microsoft® Word in *The Nelson Handwriting Font* of your choice. Select all and go to the *Format* option on the toolbar, click *Font*, change the size to 650 point and choose the Outline option in the *Effects* menu. This has been done for you in **Resource Sheet 9, Enlarged Alphabet Cards**.

Activity
Ask the children to sit in a circle and place the letter cards in the middle. Invite one child to pick a card and hold it up for the circle to see. Encourage all the children to sing the alphabet song, but when they get to the letter being held up, they have to clap their hands (or carry out any other action). At the end of the alphabet song write the letter in the air with the children, at first with their eyes open and then closed.

Alternatively, they can practise writing the letter on another child's back with their fingers. Choose another child to pick a letter and repeat the activity.

Preparation
- You will need a set of large (A4 or A3) laminated alphabet cards, with several copies of all the cards.
- To create these enter each letter of the alphabet into Microsoft® Word in the NT Font of your choice. Select all and go to the *Format* option on the tool bar, click *Font*, change the size to 650 point. This has been done for you in **Resource Sheet 9, Enlarged Alphabet Cards,** but you may wish to remove the outline effect, by selecting all, going to *Format*, *Font*, and deselecting the outline box.
- For the more challenging version of this activity replace the letters with a combination of letters which make a particular sound, e.g. **ch, sh, th, ea, oo**.

Activity
In a large space place the cards face up, but in no particular order on the floor. Ask the children to space themselves out around the letters and explain that they will have to move around the space when music is playing. When the music stops they have to go to the card with the first letter of their names. The next time ask the children to look for the card with the second letter of their names, and so on.

To make this activity more difficult ask the children to look for the first letter of their best friend's name, mother's name, sibling's name. Tip: Don't tell the children what letter they are looking for until they have stopped.

Extra: Use this activity in PE as a warm up activity, in literacy as a handwriting activity, or as part of a maths oral/mental starter substituting the letters for numbers.

6 How do you feel?

- To begin to understand how people feel.
- Cross-curricular: PSHE
- For the whole class.

Preparation

- Make a chart with every child's name in one column and a second column for putting a badge/label that says how the child feels.
- Create word labels featuring words children would use to describe their emotions.
- Laminate the words and stick Blu-Tack to them.

Activity

When the children come in, in the morning (or at any time of the day) encourage them to take one of the labels and place it by their names. This is a great starting point for PSHE work as it encourages the children to think about their feeling and others.

On a class, group or on an individual bases, discuss how the children have said they feel and ask why they feel this way. You could ask children to suggest what they might do to change the way the person feels or how their behaviour could help others. This gives the children an opportunity to talk about the things that are important to them.

Alternatively, the children could have a selection of badges to choose from daily and they wear that badge for a period of time. The badge could say 'Today I feel …' and the child can choose the word that best describes his/her feeling and write it on. If the badges are laminated the children can a use a whiteboard pen for writing their feelings so that it can be rubbed out and reused. The children could also be asked to form pairs to discuss each other's badges.

7 Peg badges

- To learn to use different fonts and how to type.
- Cross curricular: ICT
- For the whole class.

Preparation

- Set up a template for the children to type their names into for their peg badge. See **Resource Sheet 7, Name Badge Layout** as an example.
- Ensure the *Nelson Handwriting Options* menu is available and that the Outline effect is selected by going to the *Format* menu, clicking on *Font* and ticking Outline.

Activity

Invite each child to type out their name in one of the *Nelson Handwriting* fonts, to print it and cut it out. Alternatively, they could insert some Clip Art.

The children can then colour in their name and draw a picture of themselves.

Laminate each tag and make a hole at the top of the tag. Thread an elastic band through this hole and secure. This tag can be carried on though the school with them.

3 USING *THE NELSON HANDWRITING FONT* IN KEY STAGE 1

HINTS AND TIPS

 Worksheets

Create your own worksheets to focus on any of the joins that the children are learning at the time. The children could use the software to type out the joins that they find difficult and create their own worksheets to practise with.

See **Resource Sheets 1-6** as examples or use these as templates to design your own.

Homework sheets

Design a homework sheet for the sound you have learnt that week, e.g. **ew**, **ch**, **th**.

Make a table with three columns, fill the first row with three different sounds and set the children the challenge of finding as many words as they can that have those sounds in them.

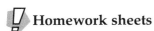

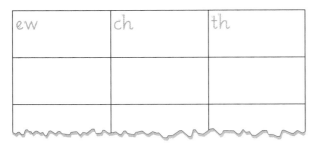

ew	ch	th

Washing line for maths

Print a selection of labels for the days of the week and months of the year. Ask the children to arrange them daily. See **Wordlist 2** for Numeracy vocabulary that has been entered for you.

Key word cards or tricky word cards

Type out a selection of these words in the appropriate font option and laminate the cards for the children to use on their tables when they are writing. See **Wordlist 1, NLS Words** for High Frequency vocabulary that has been entered for you.

Diaries

The children could make a diary to use in the playground and at home.

The diary could be done as part of an ICT lesson and the children could be encouraged to design a front cover and a first page that contains their personal details such as name, address and date of birth. The children could then use the diaries for recording anything they wish both at home and at school. The entries could be shared as part of their PSHE.

Pattern, letter and word walls

Use a low-level display board to stick lots of enlarged (A3) letter patterns, joins, phonics clusters or words. Invite the children to use crayons, paint brushes and paint or any other drawing material and trace the pattern, or copy it underneath on tramlines.

Provide extra support by placing a box of laminated pattern or letter cards next to the display. The children can select a card and copy the pattern or individual letter.

Alternatively, print the letters or letter patterns and photocopy them onto acetate sheets. Stick these on the windows. Repeat the above activity. Do this regularly to encourage writing and generate a great display for reference and achievement.

How many words can you think of to do with ... ?

Use this as a warm up activity, as an extra activity for early finishers, or as a literacy lesson.

Ask the children to think of as many words as they can that relate to a particular topic. Example: weight for maths, or space for science. Get the children to make labels of these words and use them to start a topic display. The whole class can use these to learn key words relating to topics, while you can use this as an assessment tool at the start of a topic to gauge how much a pupil already knows about the topic.

ACTIVITIES

1 Follow that Pattern

- To develop fine and gross motor skills.
- To produce a controlled line which supports letter formation.
- For groups or the whole class.

Preparation
- Prepare a selection of resource sheets for each group which feature the start of letter patterns within tramlines. For example:

- To create these, use the NT Precursive or NT Cursive font to repeat a letter and form a pattern. Highlight this text and add tramlines using the *Nelson Handwriting Options Menu*. Try using **Resource Sheet 8, Gross Motor Skill Patterns** as a starting point.
- Leave some blank space on each line for the children to continue the pattern on their own.
- Print these out, and enlarge to A3 size on the photocopier if you prefer.
- Alternatively, this activity could be done with small groups on an interactive whiteboard.

Activity
Give one resource sheet to each group and demonstrate how to start the pattern. Explain to the children that the objective is to make their pattern as close to the original as possible.

Invite one child to start the pattern in the group and then call 'Change', beat a drum or clap, and ask the child to pass on the sheet to child sitting next to them. Continue until everyone has had a turn. Invite the children to evaluate/discuss who has been most successful and why. They could also swap with another group and look at which one is the closest in this group. Each table could vote for which groups they thought was the best.

Support: To make this easier create the pattern across the whole line and ask the children to trace over it.

Challenge: To make it more difficult give the children a resource sheet of empty tramlines and ask them to copy the pattern you demonstrated on the board or in the air.

2 Let's join our letters!

- To begin using and practising the four basic handwriting joins.
- For the whole class, groups or individuals.

Preparation
- Create a set of cards featuring each letter of the alphabet. You can type them into a table, cut them out and laminate them. Use **Resource Sheet 10, Alphabet Cards** as a template for this.

Activity
Depending on the joins you are teaching at the time, place the relevant cards in front of the children. Invite a child to pick a card and another child to pick a second card. Display the cards and ask the children to decide, in pairs, how to join the two letters. Encourage the children to practise this on their whiteboards before inviting some to come the board to demonstrate. The teacher can then demonstrate to confirm correct join and the children copy/practice.

3 Let's join our letters on the whiteboard!

- To begin using and practising the four basic handwriting joins.
- For whole class and group work.

Preparation

- Enter the pattern or join that you are focusing on the interactive whiteboard in the Grey Font option (this shows start dots and directional arrows)

- The children can trace over the letters with their finger, or a pen but if you want them to make visible marks you will need to make sure you activate Active Studio.

- See **Wordlist 5, Handwriting Words** for tables of words featuring the 4 different joins.

Activity

Introduce/reinforce the appropriate joins by tracing over them with your pen/finger. As you do this, invite the children to sky write these shapes/joins or come up to the board to try it themselves.

This particularly supports children with less developed motor skills and will assist their letter formation and in developing accurate joining. Provide the children with on-screen tramlines so they can progress to scribing next to the words typed in the font.

Challenge: Invite the children to try writing words first, and then using the NT Font to check they have formed their joins correctly.

4 Who has the same sound?

- To practise and revise previously learnt phonemes. To learn knew phonemes.
- For the whole class.

Preparation

- Create phoneme cards based on what the children have learnt so far, enlarge them so there is one sound per A4 page and laminate them.

Activity

Give each child a card and give some children the same sound but made up of different letters, e.g. **ow**, **ou** or **oa**, **o**, **ow**. Say one of the sounds out loud, for example **o**, and ask all the children with cards that make that sound to form one group, and the rest of the children to form another group.

As the children get better at this game, introduce more sounds per game. For example, you can give cards that make **o** sounds, cards that make **ee** sounds, cards that make **ou** sounds, and cards with different sounds. They should then form the groups that you have asked them to; eg a group of **ee** sounds, **ou** sounds or **oo** sounds. This will encourage the children to discuss their cards with others and really focus on their sound and shape.

Challenge: After this game, focus on one of the sounds and invite the children to write words with that sound on small whiteboards. They could also construct a sentence on their whiteboards or decide a sentence with a partner and share it with the class.

4 Spot the mistake!

- To learn correct letter orientation, formation and proportion.

- For whole class.

Preparation
- Create a selection of letters/words on tramlines to support your handwriting focus. See **Wordlist 5** for words containing the different joins that have been entered for you.

- Print the selection.

Activity
Give one printout to each child, pair or group. Demonstrate writing one of the letters/words on the board on tramlines, making some mistakes. Encourage the children to put a tick, cross or comment by the letter/word on their sheet to show whether they think you have formed the letter correctly or not.

As a class, invite the children to discuss what each other thought and then reveal if it is correct or not.

Demonstrate this again (correctly) and ask the children to copy in the air and then on their paper.

 Extra: This activity could be done on an inter-active whiteboard.

6 Let's learn about letters!

- A warm up activity to explore letter shapes and how letters are formed and joined.

- For the whole class.

Preparation
- You will need a set of large (A4 or A3) alphabet cards.

- To create these enter each letter of the alphabet into Word in *The Nelson Handwriting Font* of your choice. Select all and select the *Format* option on the toolbar, click *Font*, change the size to 400 point and choose the Outline option in the *Effects* menu. This has been done for you in **Resource Sheet 9, Enlarged Alphabet Cards**.

Learning about letters

33

Activity

Try using this activity as a warm up before a handwriting focus on particular letter shapes or joins. You can then move on to practising these letters or joins on their whiteboards or in their books.

Give each child a card with a letter of the alphabet (some children can have the same letter, depending on the class size). In a large space, ask the children to arrange themselves into groups of:

- Letters with ascenders and descenders.
- Letters that are written clockwise or anticlock-wise.
- Letters that are written using the **c** pattern.
- Letters that are written using the **r** pattern.
- Letters that join horizontally and those that join diagonally.
- Letters that join horizontally with ascenders and descenders.
- Letters that join diagonally with and without ascenders.
- Or a combination of any of these.

Remember to create a separate group for the children that don't fit into any of the above groups.

7 Bingo

- To learn letters, sounds and words.
- For groups or the whole class.

Preparation

- Make a 3 x 3 grid A4 size and place a letter, sound or word in each box. Each child, pair or group will need a whiteboard with different sounds or a different arrangement of the same sounds on their card.

- Use **Resource Sheet 11, Bingo Card** as a template. Laminate these for future use.

- You will also need whiteboard markers. If these are not available then do not laminate the bingo cards, simply photocopy them and use pencils.

- Create a set of letter, sound or word cards that match the ones you have put onto the children's bingo cards for the bingo caller. (These are optional as you could simply select your own bingo results if you wish to focus on particular letters sounds or words.)

For example:

ay	oo	ch
st	igh	ll
ue	ing	ee

Activity

Give each child, pair or table a bingo card that you have prepared. The teacher chooses a card from a pile and calls out the sound, or word/letter on it. If the children have the same as the teacher they should write over it. The first to complete three in a row wins.

 Extra: Invite the winning child/team to demonstrate the joins on the whiteboard.

8 Talking about Tramlines

- To learn how to form letters in proportion, and where to position them on the lines.

- For the whole class, or groups.

Preparation
- Set up the interactive whiteboard in Microsoft® Word.

- Ensure the children have small writing boards and pens

Activity
Type a letter or word on the whiteboard and ask the children to discuss where they think the letters would be if they were on tramlines. For example, a child might say that the letter **a** would be inside the middle lines, or a **b** would start in the middle lines but it would have an ascender up to the top line.

Highlight the word or letter and select *Nelson Handwriting Options*, and then Tramlines to add tramlines. The children can then see the correct position.

Ask the children to practise writing the letter or word on their own whiteboards.

FURTHER ACTIVITIES FOR USE ACROSS THE CURRICULUM

1 Designing and Making

- To use a range of presentational skills

- To learn how to keep healthy and about hygiene – PSHE.

Activity

Discuss with the children the best way of planning a poster, suggesting ideas like brainstorming, sketching the layout, using bullet points, capital letters and other presentation issues.

Introduce the topic for the poster, in this case rules for the toilet area. Encourage the children to brainstorm what these rules should be, such as always flush the toilet and to remember to wash their hands, based on previous discussions.

Invite the children to plan their poster, once they have decided which rules they should include and to make a poster on the PC.

Extra: Encourage the children to design and make other posters for the classroom, playground or the school as a whole or which extend to other areas of the curriculum.

2 PSHE and ICT

- To insert images and to present text.

- For the whole class.

Activity

Invite the children to make a 'Most wanted' poster, using as many fonts available, including those in the *Nelson Handwriting Options*.

Encourage them to type their name, age, eye colour, hair colour and a statement about themselves.

If you have a digital camera they could insert a picture of themselves, or simply draw themselves. Use their posters to make a display in the class.

3 QCA Science 'Ourselves'

- To learn the parts of the body.

Activity

Make a large display of the human body. This could be done by asking the children to trace round each other. They could then make labels to stick next to the right body parts. You could make this an interactive display by taking the labels down daily so that the children find the right place to stick them on again.

**4 QCA Science 'Materials'
QCA History 'Houses and
Homes'**

- To learn the names of different types of
homes.

Activity

Create a large display of different types of homes.
This could be made with pictures you have
collected or templates cut out of card. The
children make and stick on labels saying where
the different materials would be found. They can
also do this for the different types of houses,
bungalow, terraced … Once again, the children
can do this daily at the end of a lesson or during
their morning activity, if the teacher takes down
the display.

**5 QCA Geography 'Around
Our School'**

- To learn their address and to learn
about the process of writing and sending
a letter.

Activity

In this unit the children learn about the postal
system. They write a letter to their parents/
guardians at home and post it. In order for
children to have a readable address which
doesn't detract from the main point of the
activity, you could copy their addresses in a
Microsoft® Word document from the schools
record and then covert it into cursive Grey Font.
The children can then write over this and stick
the label or piece of paper on their envelope.

**6 QCA Geography 'How to
Make your Local Area Safer'**

- To write labels for displays and to learn
the about road safety.

Activity

In this topic the children take photographs of
roads, traffic lights, pelican crossings, and so on.
They then should make labels for the different
things in the photographs. This could be done
using the NT Precursive script or Grey Text for
children who need the extra support. This could
take place during a handwriting session or be
part of the literacy lesson on making labels for
displays.

**7 QCA Science 'Growing
Plants'**

- To learn the parts of flowers.

Activity

Draw a flower and ask the children to make
labels for the petals, roots, stem and leaves.
Laminate these and leave them on display for
the children to label.

4 USING *THE NELSON HANDWRITING FONT* IN KEY STAGE 2

HINTS AND TIPS

Model texts

In Key Stage 2 it is useful to provide examples of text types in *The Nelson Handwriting Font,* alongside any other good examples of joined handwriting. This reminds the writers of the joins and standards to aim for.

Handwriting Targets

Introduce a simple achievable handwriting target at the publishing stage of the writing process to assess progress and motivate the writers.

For example, use statements from the NLS Handwriting objectives, such as:

Remember to use:
- diagonal joins to letters without ascenders, e.g. **ai**, **ar**, **un**;

- horizontal joins to letters without ascenders, e.g. **ou**, **vi**, **wi**;

- diagonal joins to letters with ascenders, e.g. **ab**, **ul**, **it**;

- horizontal joins to letters with ascenders, e.g. **ol**, **wh**, **ot**.

Make sure your handwriting is:
- consistent in size and proportions;

- has consistent spacing between letters and words.

Know when to:
- use a clear neat hand for finished, presented work;

- use informal writing for everyday informal work, rough drafting, etc;

- build up speed, e.g. particularly for notes, drafts, lists;

- to use a range of presentational skills, e.g. print script for captions, subheadings and labels; capital letters for posters, title pages, headings; a range of computer-generated fonts and point sizes.

Worksheets

Make a selection of worksheets that focus on any of the joins that the children are learning at the time. This is particularly useful for pupils who need extra support because you can ensure that the worksheets are at the correct interest level for your pupil.

Use **Resource Sheets 1-6** as templates to design your own. Alternatively, invite the children to use the software to type out the joins that they find difficult and create their own worksheets to practise. (See page 22 for more guidance on this.)

How to use *The Nelson Handwriting Font* to reinforce your spelling strategies at KS2

You can use *The Nelson Handwriting Font* to support many of the *NLS Spelling Bank* activities, which will help link handwriting and spelling practice. In addition, when children are learning to spell new and challenging words, encourage them to play with these words on a PC in *The Nelson Handwriting Font* in a cursive option. They can pull compound words apart, use different colours to highlight prefixes and suffixes and explore the joins within the words too. Encourage them to take turns to type their spelling tips and ideas using the NT Cursive and NT Cursive Slanted. You may wish the children to practise by copying the ideas into their own spelling logs, or by printing and pasting them in.

Words within words

Encourage children to highlight words they find within words, and to share this with their group or partner. Ask them to create sentences to help them to remember how to spell the words.

For example: **hear** —
you **hear** *with your ear*

Handwriting in action.

LSCWC

Use *The Nelson Handwriting Font* to create wordlists for the children to consolidate their spelling. The NT Cursive font will reinforce the visual image of the word, which is particularly useful when teaching the children to use the **Look–Say–Cover–Write–Check** strategy.

Mnemonics

Challenge the children to create their own mnemonics for remembering words they find difficult to spell. They can try doing this on a PC using *The Nelson Handwriting Font* to experiment with lots of different words, and using the dictionary and thesaurus functionality to support them. For example:

Big elephants can always understand small elephants – Because

ACTIVITIES

1 Pick and Mix

- To practise joins between sets of letters.
- For pairs and small groups.

Preparation
- Prepare letter cards featuring sets 1 to 4 and the break letters in the NT Cursive font, one letter per card. Use **Resource Sheets 12, Joining Sets** to support this.

- Have whiteboards or handwriting books, a PC or an interactive whiteboard and counters for team points available.

Activity
1 Arrange each set of cards face down on the table.

2 Children take turns to turn over one letter from each set being practised – set 1 to 2, set 1 to 3, set 4 to 2, set 4 to 3 or the break letters.

3 The other team or partner writes and joins the letters chosen.

4 The opposition checks the join by typing the letters in the NT Cursive font.

5 Counters are given as a reward for accurate joins. The team with the most counters at the end of the game wins.

Challenge: Choose from more than two sets or give each team a word to spell and join instead.

2 Bingo

- To reinforce skills and joins from handwriting lesson.
- For small groups or the whole class.

Preparation
- Use the Nelson Handwriting Cursive font to create cards featuring the joins you are focusing on in the handwriting lesson, one join per card. See **Resource Sheet 12, Joining Sets** to support this.

- Have available a list of joins being practised on the whiteboard for children to choose from.

- The children will need small whiteboards to use as bingo cards.

Activity
1 Ask the children to write down four or six of the joins being practised on their whiteboards to make a bingo card.

2 Shuffle the cards.

3 Ask the bingo caller to hold up each card displaying the join.

4 The children score off the letter joins on their whiteboards as they are held up.

5 The winner is the first person to score off each letter join on their whiteboard.

6 Invite the winner to demonstrate how to join the letters that appeared on his/her bingo card.

Challenge: You could adapt this game for the phonemes and digraphs being practised in spelling work. Instead of showing the letters, the bingo caller calls the phonemes, combining phonics and handwriting.

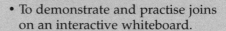

3 Tracing Frenzy

- To reinforce work in handwriting lessons.

- For individuals in need of further support.

Preparation
- Create worksheets featuring the letters being practised, or an illustrative sentence, typed in the NT Cursive or NT Grey font.

You will need:
- Acetate or tracing paper
- Dry wipe pens or handwriting pens
- Sand timer or stop clock.

Activity
Ask the children to trace over the worksheets onto the acetate or tracing paper.

Encourage the children to complete the task in the time given, using the sand timer to motivate them.

Challenge: Vary the size of the font and allow the children to practise with and without tramlines.

4 Interactive copying

- To demonstrate and practise joins on an interactive whiteboard.

- For whole class, groups or individuals.

Activity
During a handwriting lesson you can use *The Nelson Handwriting Font* to:

- demonstrate and practise joins;

- encourage the children to copy the font using the interactive pen;

- trace the NT Cursive font, perhaps in a different colour or finger-write over it;

- practise speedwriting, printing, and developing different styles;

- experiment with different sizes of font, with and without tramlines.

See **Resource Sheet 12** to support this.

Support: Left-handers may find this very rewarding because they won't smudge the ink as they push through the joins.

5 Speedwriting

- To encourage readable fluent handwriting.
- For pairs or two small teams.

 Extra: Encourage the children to calculate their handwriting speed using the following formula.

$$\frac{\text{Numbers of letters written}}{\text{Number of minutes taken}} = \text{writing speed (in letters per minute)}$$

My writing speed is ☐ letters per minute

Alternatively, play the game on a standard whiteboard with sentences enlarged in the NT Cursive font, printed on acetate and projected on the board, or printed on paper and stuck to the board.

Preparation
- Save a list of sentences or spelling words for the teams to use on the interactive whiteboard in the Nelson handwriting cursive font.
- You will need a stop clock and small whiteboards for all children to speed write.
- Arrange the class or group into teams.

Activity
1 Invite a child from one of the teams to come to the whiteboard. Show them the sentence they have to copy, and encourage them to write the sentence out as quickly as they can. Remind the children that it doesn't have to be their neatest writing, but is has to be readable.

2 While they are doing this, ask the other team to time them using the stop clock. Keep a record of how long it took them.

3 Team members can then alternate at the whiteboard, trying to beat the opposing team's time to write the sentence.

4 The team with the fastest writers at the end, wins.

5 The children not being timed practise writing the same sentence onto their small white-boards.

6 Make a word

- To practise joins and spelling objectives.
- For pairs, small groups or the whole class.

Preparation
- Enter and save parts of words or root words, that relate to your spelling work, using the NT Cursive template in Microsoft® Word on the interactive whiteboard.

- Ensure children have small whiteboards and dry wipe pens for all children to practise and dictionaries to hand to check new words made.

Activity
Display parts of words or root words that relate to your handwriting or spelling work on the interactive whiteboard. Encourage the children to take turns to add to the word to make a new word, by using the interactive pen to join to the root word on the interactive whiteboard, or by entering the words on the keyboard.

For example:
Add to the root word – *destruct* to make *destructible*

The next person adds to the word – *in* to make *indestructible*

Ask the other children playing to add to the word on their own whiteboards, joining correctly. Encourage the children to check the new words made in the dictionaries and to check that the joins they have made are correct by typing the word in the Nelson Handwriting Cursive Font.

NB If joins within words seem to be inaccurate when pulling letter combinations together, highlight the whole word and select NT Cursive or NT Cursive Slanted from the *Options* menu, to refresh the joins.

Challenge: You may wish to use the words given in the Developing Skills books, or link it to work in literacy, e.g. adding a prefix or suffix.

7 Word jumble

- To practise any spelling objective.
- For individuals or pairs working together.

Preparation
- Use *The Nelson Handwriting Font* to make anagrams/conundrums of words being practised in spelling sessions.

- Either photocopy for individuals and pairs, or save onto the interactive whiteboard.

Activity
Ask the children to unscramble the letters to find words relevant to their word level work. Encourage the children to **look–say–cover–write –check** the words using joined handwriting.

Extra: Try using **Resource Sheet 12, Joining Sets** here, to focus on words which include the joins you are specifically teaching in your handwriting focus.

8 Compound word match

- To practise recognising and spelling compound words.
- For pairs or small groups.

Preparation
- Use the Nelson Handwriting Font to make cards with a selection of base words.

Activity

1 Arrange the cards face down on the table.

2 Ask the children to take turns to turn over two cards.

3 If the two words turned over make a compound word, the child keeps the pair.

4 The child with the most compound words at the end of the game, wins.

5 Encourage the children to copy the compound words in their spelling logs, using joined handwriting.

Challenge: Ask the children to generate compound words using the NT Cursive font, to be printed and split before the game is played. It could be offered to another group working on the same activity.

5 TROUBLESHOOTING

Nearly all of the standard Microsoft® Word functionality works with the Nelson Handwriting Font. There are some exceptions to this which are detailed below.

Selecting Fonts

Please select the handwriting fonts by going to the *Nelson Handwriting Options* menu. If you select the handwriting fonts from the drop down menu in Word, the letters will not join correctly.

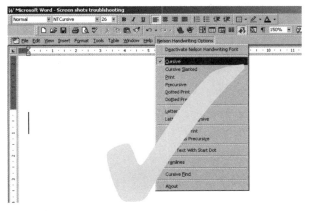

Select from here ...

... do not select from here.

Using tables and text boxes

If you try to create a table in the Handwriting Font template you will notice that the cursor behaves unpredictably. This can be controlled with the following steps:

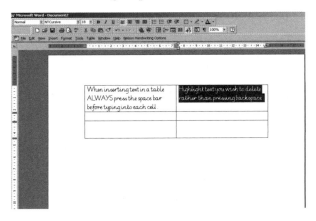

- Before keying any Cursive text into a table or text box, always press the space bar once. If you forget to do this, the order of the letters may invert.

- Do not try to highlight the entire table and pre-select a handwriting font. Instead, either separately highlight the text in each table cell and select your font, or select your font before you start typing.

- If you need to delete text in a table, highlight the whole cell and select *Delete*. If you use the backspace key, the cursor may jump back to the previous cell.

Using tramlines

The simplest way to add tramlines to text is to:

- Highlight existing text (which must be in one of the handwriting fonts – not a commercial font). Go to the *Nelson Handwriting Options* window and select *Tramlines*.

- Tramlines will appear around the text. Now immediately go back to the drop-down window and deselect *Tramlines*.

If you wish to create blank tramlines for children to write in please use the following steps:

- Move the cursor to a new line and select 'Tramlines' as described above, ensuring you have a handwriting font and the desired size of the tramlines selected.

- Press the Tab key and blank tramlines will appear on your page.

- If you wish to produce several rows of empty tramlines, at the end of each line please press *Enter* to start a new line rather than continually pressing tab. Otherwise the tramlines will disappear.

Please note, to create space after words in tramlines use the tab key rather than the space bar.

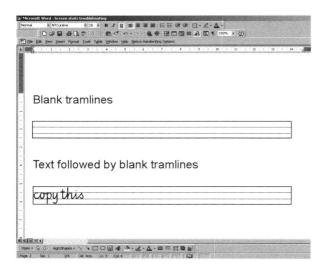

Using bullet points

Do not type in real time with Microsoft® Word's bullet point function selected. Instead, first create the text to which you wish to add bullet points/numbers, highlight it and then add bullet points retrospectively.

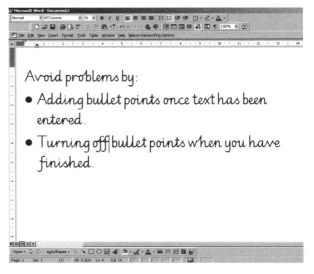

Automatic Spelling and Grammar checking

Installing *The Nelson Handwriting Font* will switch any automatic spelling and grammar checkers off. These can be turned back on again, if desired, by selecting *Tools> Options> Spelling and Grammar* then ticking the appropriate check boxes.

Please Note:

If you've been working on a document for a while and start to experience difficulties, save your changes, close the file and then reopen it to 'refresh' the screen.

If you have any difficulties or problems, please contact our technical support helpline on 01242 267383.

6 ONLINE RESOURCES

These editable Resource Sheets and Word Lists are available at:
www.nelsonthornes.com/nelsonhandwritingfont. See pages 4-5 for a full list of resources.

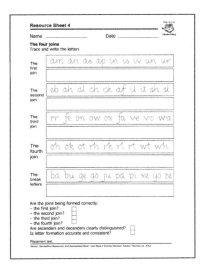

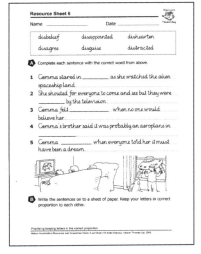

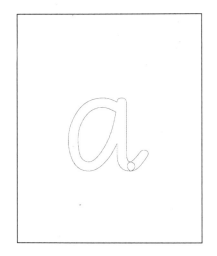

a	b	c	d	e
f	f	g	h	i
j	k	k	l	m

Set 1

a	c	d	e	h	i
k	l	m	n	s	t
u					

Handwriting words:

clockwise	anticlockwise
vertical	horizontal
ascender	descender
diagonal	parallel
consonant	vowel
joined	sloped
x-height	speedwriting

NLS Reception High Frequency Words

a	all	am	and
are	at	away	big
can	cat	come	dad
day	dog	for	get
go	going	he	I
in	is	it	like
look	me	mum	my
no	of	on	play
said	see	she	the
they	this	to	up
was	we	went	yes
you			

NLS Y1-2 High Frequency Words

about	after		
again	an	another	as
back	ball	be	because
bed	been	boy	brother
but	by	call	called
came	can't	could	did
dig	do	don't	door
down	first	from	girl
good	got	had	half
has	have	help	her
here	him	his	home

Numeracy

add	addition	anticlockwise	calculate
calculation	centimetre	centre	circle
clockwise	compare	cube	cuboid
cylinder	diamond	double	eight
eighteen	eighty	eleven	estimate
fifteen	fifty	five	forty
four	fourteen	fraction	graph
group	guess	half	halve
hexagon	hundred	kilogram	left
less	litre	make	match
measure	million	nearest	negative
nine	nineteen	ninety	oblong
octagon	one	opposite	oval
pair	pattern	pentagon	pictogram
pointed	positive	pyramid	quarter
rectangle	reflection	round	rule
sequence	set	seven	seventeen
seventy	shape	shapes	six
sixteen	sixty	size	sort
sphere	square	star	sum
symmetrical	tally	ten	tens
thirteen	thirty	thousand	three
total	triangle	twelve	twenty
twenty-one	two	units	zero

Colours

black			
blue	brown	colour	colours
dark	gold	green	grey
indigo	light	orange	pink
purple	red	silver	turquoise
violet	white	yellow	

Classroom

apron	aprons	bell	blocks
board	book	books	chair
chairs	chalk	children	clock
computer	crayon	crayons	desk
door	drawer	dressing up	glue
hall	keyboard	Lego	library
light	mobile	mouse	paint
paintbrush	paintbrushes	paints	paper
peg	pen	pencil	pencils
pens	printer	rubber	ruler
scissors	screen	switch	table
tables	tap	teacher	toilet
trains	wall	water	whistle
whiteboard	window		

Girls' names

Abigail			
Ailsa	Aisha	Alana	Ali
Alice	Alicia	Amy	Anna
April	Ayesha	Azhar	Basimah
Beatrice	Beckie	Becky	Bethany
Bobby	Briony	Caitlin	Carol
Carole	Caroline	Carolyn	Catherine
Charlotte	Chelsea	Chloe	Claire
Clare	Cosima	Daisy	Danielle
Danni	Debbie	Debby	Deborah
Dorothy	Elayna	Eleanor	Elena
Elizabeth	Ella	Ellen	Ellie
Emily	Emma	Erica	Eve
Faridah	Francesca	Frankie	Gemma
Georgia	Hannah	Harriet	Hayfa
Hayley	Hollie	Hope	Isabelle
Jade	Jamie	Jamilah	Jane
Janet	Jenika	Jennifer	Jenny
Jessica	Jo	Joanna	Joanne
Julia	Julie	June	Kamilah
Karimah	Kate	Katherine	Kathryn
Katie	Kylie	Lara	Laura
Lauren	Leah	Lily	Lisa
Lois	Louisa	Louise	Lucy
Maddie	Madeleine	Maeve	Maggie